EDWARD ELGAR

Dream Children

Traumkinder

Op. 43

2 pieces for solo piano (1902)

2 Stücke für Klaviersolo

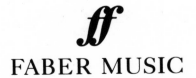

FABER MUSIC

Dream Children

No 1

EDWARD ELGAR
(1857–1934)

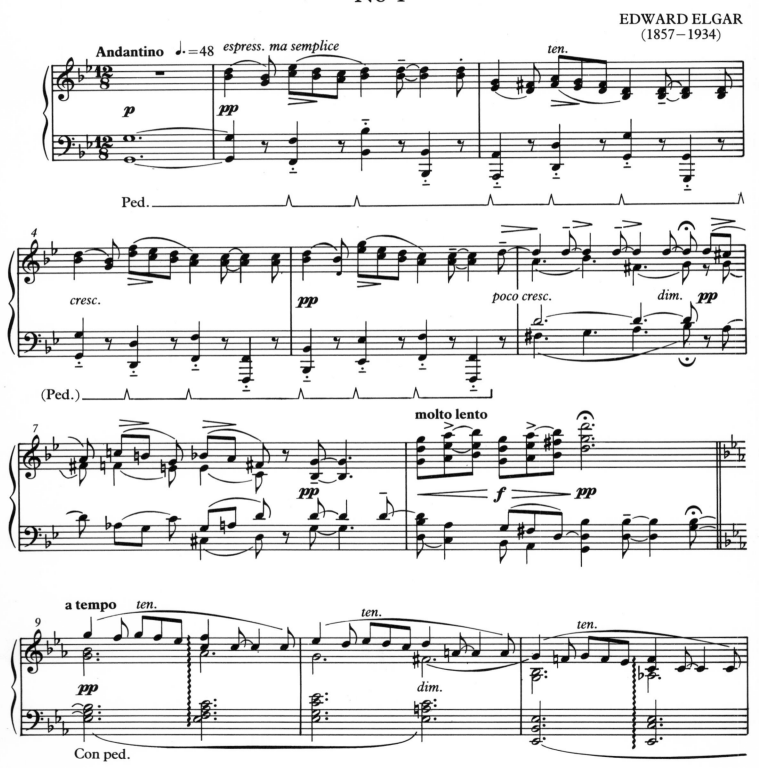

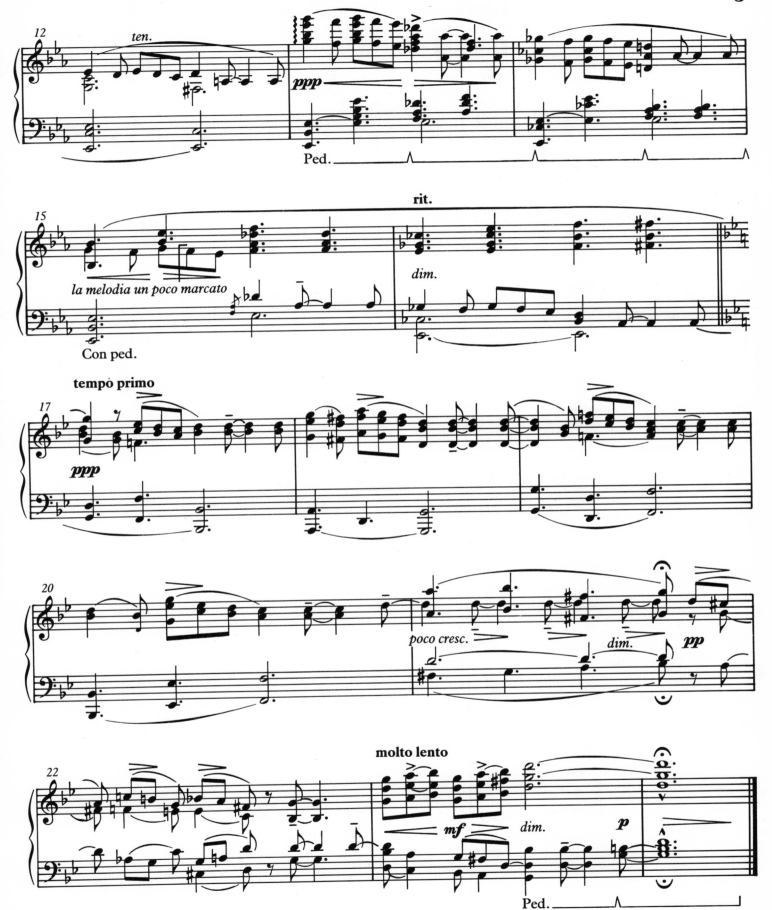

No 2

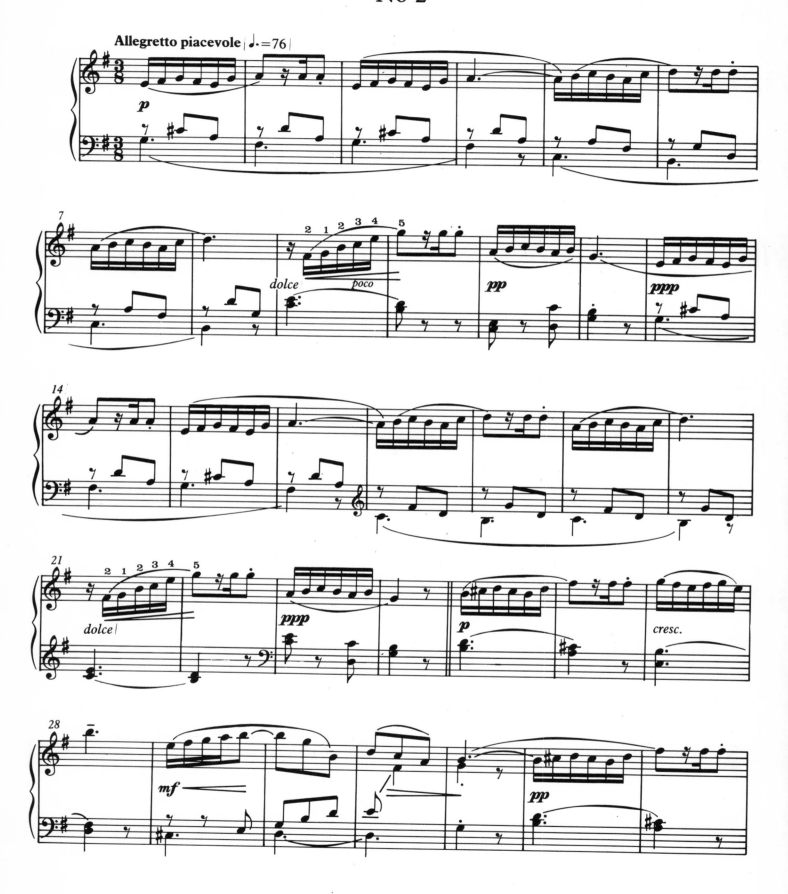

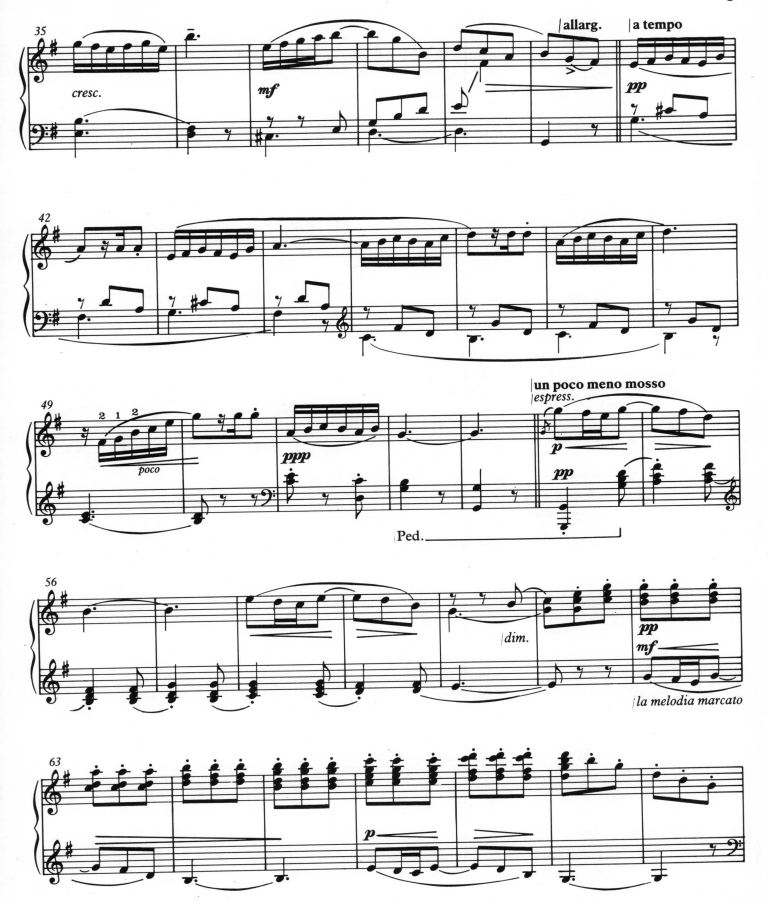

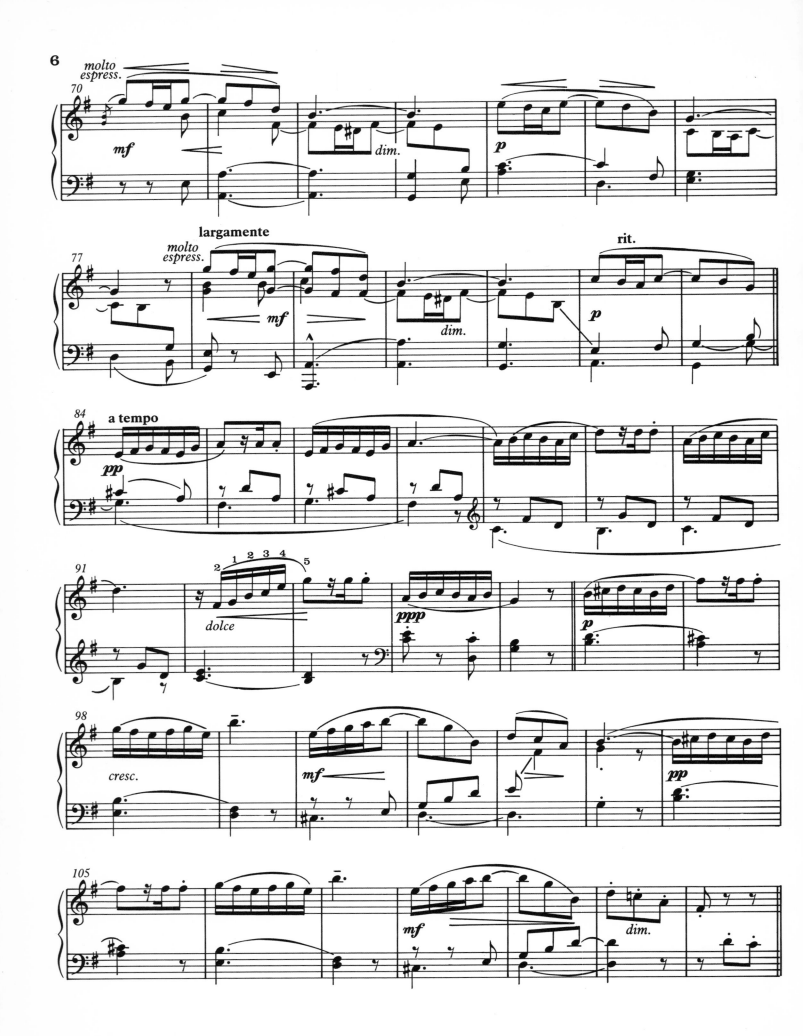

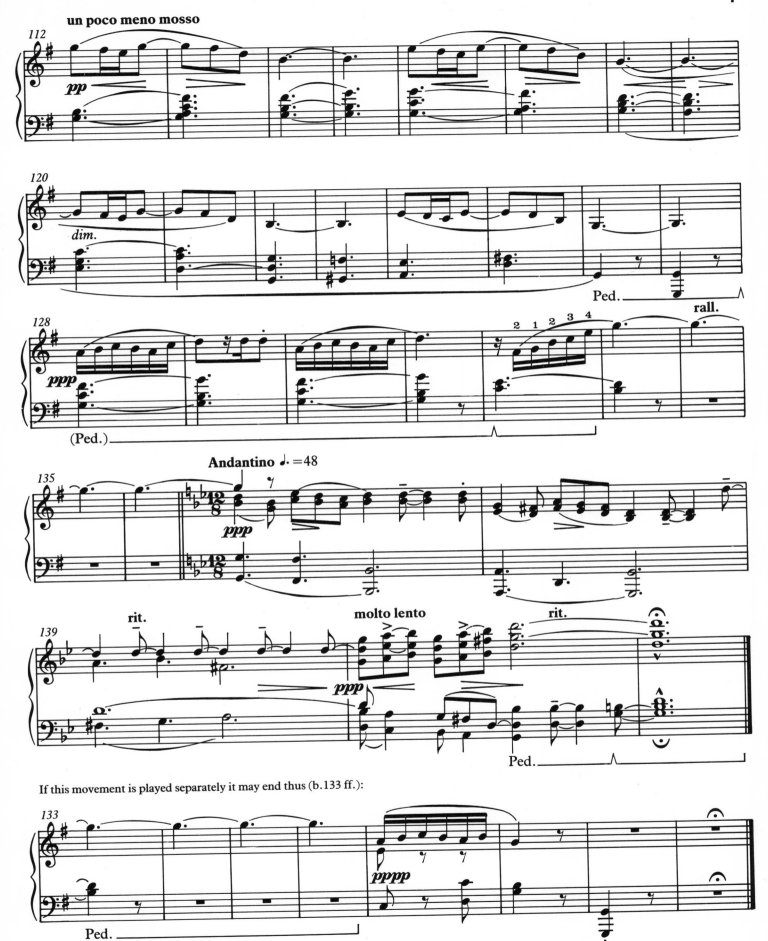

If this movement is played separately it may end thus (b.133 ff.):